THE ADULT PIANO LEVEL III

FOREWORD

This book is designed to follow logically Level II. As with Levels I and II, an earnest attempt has been made to provide the student the with materials that will satisfy his musical needs while developing a pianistic technic.

Major and minor arpeggios are introduced beginning on page 50. At this point for further arpeggio technic development, "Piano Arpeggios", Level IV, from the DAVID CARR GLOVER PIANO LIBRARY can be used.

On page 58 through 83 will be found a section devoted to original repertoire from the Baroque, Rococo, Classic Romantic, and Contemporary periods of music. For the most part this material is within the grade level that the student can perform with control. The interested student will want to go beyond the material presented in this book. If so, the teacher should guide him carefully in selecting music that is not too difficult.

A section titled, "Music For Special Occasions" will be found on pages 84 through 86. These selections have been carefully modified to approximately meet the grade level of this book. In time the student should be able to play the more difficult versions found in standard hymnals and patriotic collections. The author cautions the teacher from giving this type of music in its original version too soon, as it could, because of its difficulty, discourage the student's interest.

If correlated materials recommended with Level II have not been completed before beginning Level III, they should be continued with this third level of the Method. It is highly recommended that the student completely review all of the Method, Level II, while studying new fundamentals and pieces from this book, Level III.

The teacher should also encourage sight reading and transposition in many keys all of which will reinforce the student's knowledge, technic, and performance control.

Materials Correlated with "THE ADULT PIANO STUDENT" — Level III

IMPORTANT: Should correlated materials not be completed with the "ADULT PIANO STUDENT", Level III, continue them with the next Method Book.

F.D.L.460

Contents

c/o CPP/BELWIN, INC., Miami, Florida 33014

F.D.L.460

3

Melody

DUVERNOY

TEACHER: Suggestions for ensemble performance. 1. Have some students play the right hand melody with both hands in unison one or two octaves apart. 2. Have some students play the left hand accompaniment as written. 3. Have some students play the left hand accompaniment in chords.

Teacher: It is recommended that Adult Piano Theory, Level III, from the David Carr Glover Program for Adult Students be used at this time.

Sustained Accompaniment Studies

Sustained Accompaniment — Left Hand

Sustained Accompaniment — Left Hand

Sustained Accompaniment — Left Hand

Romance

GLOVER

Teacher: It is recommended that *Adult Piano Repertoire, Level III-A,* from the David Carr Glover Program

for Adult Students be used at this time.

F.D.L.460

At Dawn

GLOVER

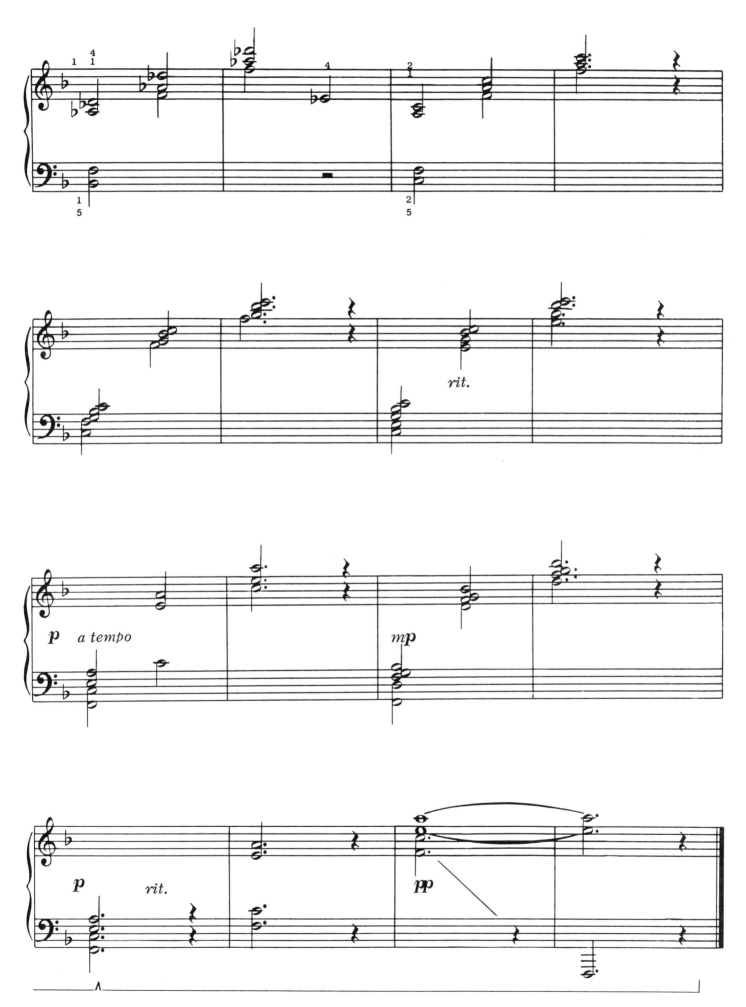

Sixteenth Notes and Sixteenth Rests

When the quarter note receives one beat, the sixteenth note receives one-fourth beat.

Sixteenth notes may be printed singly with two flags or in groups connected by a double beam.

Clap and chant the rhythm before playing the following Studies.

Keep it ev - en Keep it ev - en walk, walk, Keep it ev - en Keep it ev - en walk, walk.

Sixteenth Note Study #1

TEACHER: Studies 1 and 2 may also be played together for ensemble practice.

Sixteenth Note Study No. 2

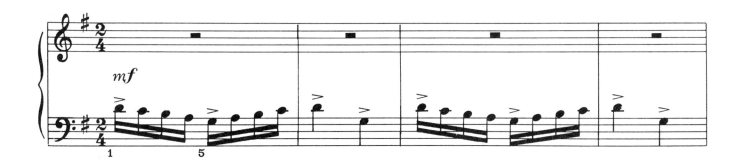

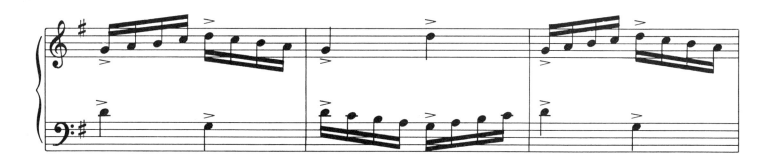

F.D.L.460

Pranks

GLOVER

Sixteenth Note Studies

Rapid Five Finger Legato, Staccato, Left Hand, E♭ Major

Rapid Five Finger Legato, Staccato, Right Hand, E♭ Major

Teacher: When the above studies have been learned hands separately, then play hands together.

F.D.L.460

Teacher: Sixteenth note studies 3, 4, and 5 may also be played together for ensemble practice.

Rapid Five Finger Legato

Rapid Five Finger Legato

Rapid Five Finger Legato, Contrary Motion

Rapid Broken and Solid Triads

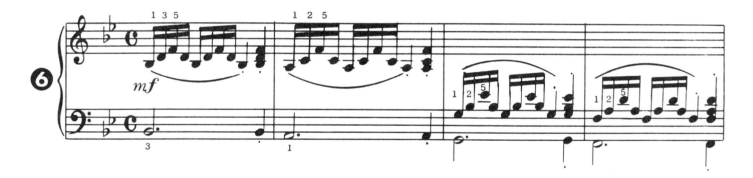

TEACHER: Study No. 6, suggestions for ensemble practice. 1. Have some students play the right hand broken chords with both hands one octave apart. 2. Have some students play the right hand broken chords as block chords with both hands one octave apart. 3. Have some students play the left hand melody with both hands in unison one or two octaves apart.

Scale Studies

TEACHER: *Scale studies 1 and 2 may also be played together for ensemble practice.*

Rapid Scales

Rapid Scales

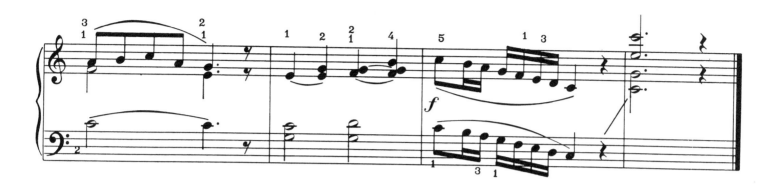

Whistling Tune

Staccato, Legato

GLOVER

F.D.L.460

Trill Study

The trill consists of the rapid alternation of two adjacent notes. When the sign of the trill appears over a note, it means that this note and the one above it are to be alternated for the time value of the printed note. In some pieces the trill figures have the notes written out, in others, the trill sign is used.

Written   **Played**

In earlier keyboard music the trill usually started on the auxiliary (upper) note.

Written   **Played**

The Trill
I

Moderato

Trill Study
II

Lively

CZERNY

Slow Dance

GRAUPNER

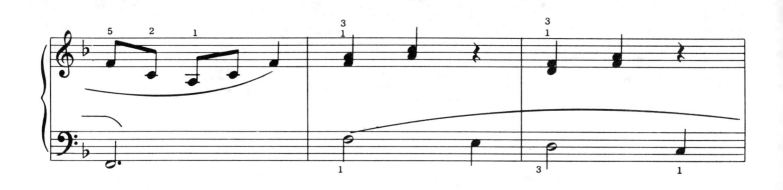

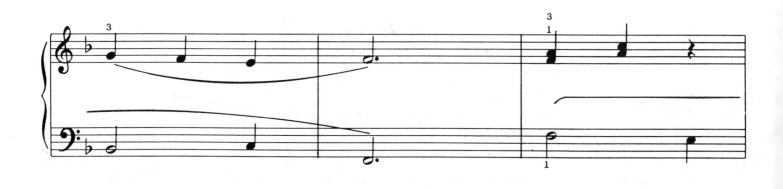

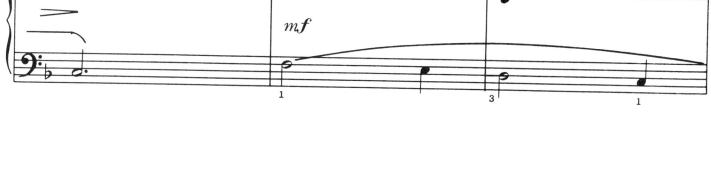

In $\frac{2}{2}$ rhythm there are two beats to each measure and a half note receives one beat.

Prelude in A♭ No. I
(Chords)

Teacher: Prelude in A♭   1 and 2 may also be played together for ensemble practice.

GLOVER

Moderato

Prelude in A♭ No. 2

Broken Chords

Moderato

GLOVER

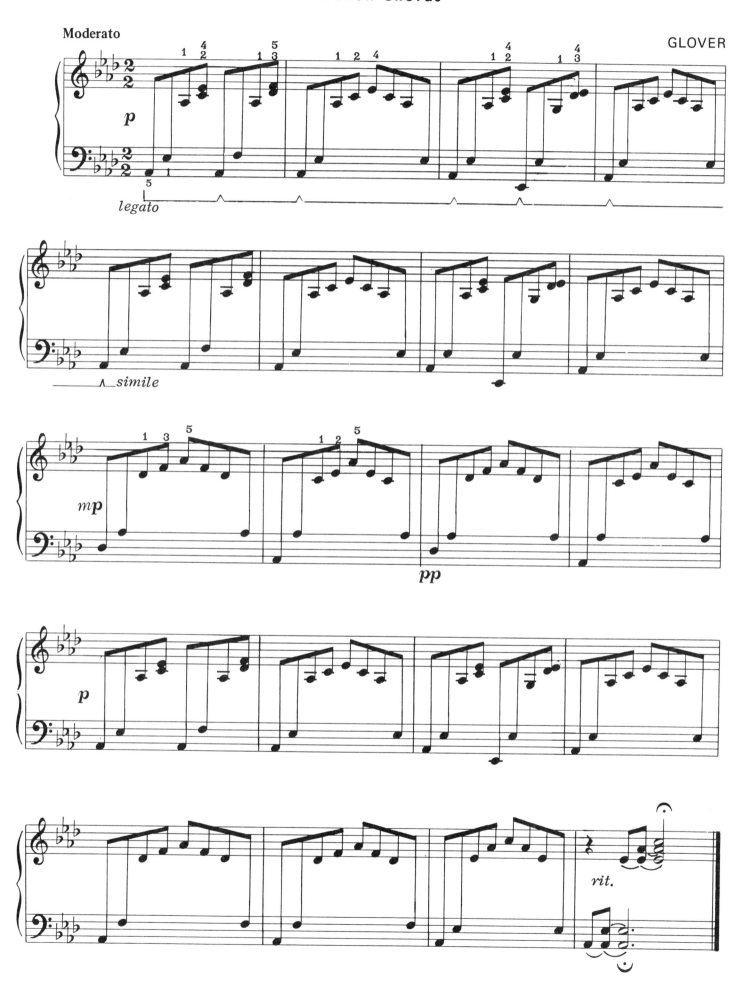

Augmented Triads

AUGMENT – TO MAKE LARGER.

When you raise the top note (5th) of a major triad ½ step, you have *augmented* the chord.

MAJOR   AUGMENTED

Augmented Etude

GLOVER

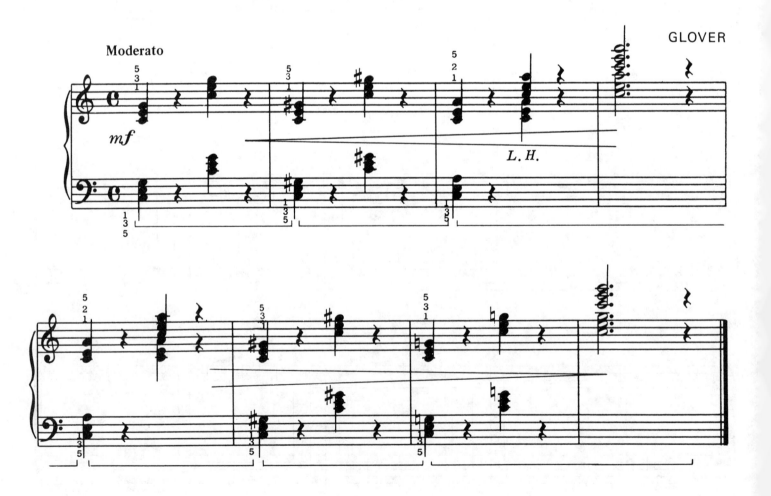

Augmented Triad Technic Studies

Prelude

GLOVER

Diminished Triads

DIMINISH — TO MAKE SMALLER.

When you lower the top note (5th) of a minor triad ½ step, you have *diminished* the chord.

MINOR   DIMINISHED

Diminished Etude

GLOVER

Moderato

mf

Diminished Triad Technic Studies

Diminished Triad and Inversions, Left Hand

Diminished Triad and Inversions, Right Hand

Diminished Triad and Inversions, Hands Together

Broken Diminished Triad and Inversions

Broken Diminished Triad and Inversions, Cross Hands

Questions-Answers

In a piece of music there are sections that seem to ask a question and sections that seem to answer the question. The question is called the Antecendent Section and the answer is called the Consequent Section.

The following piece is given with the question and answer sections marked for you. Listen carefully as you play.

Slave Ship

GLOVER

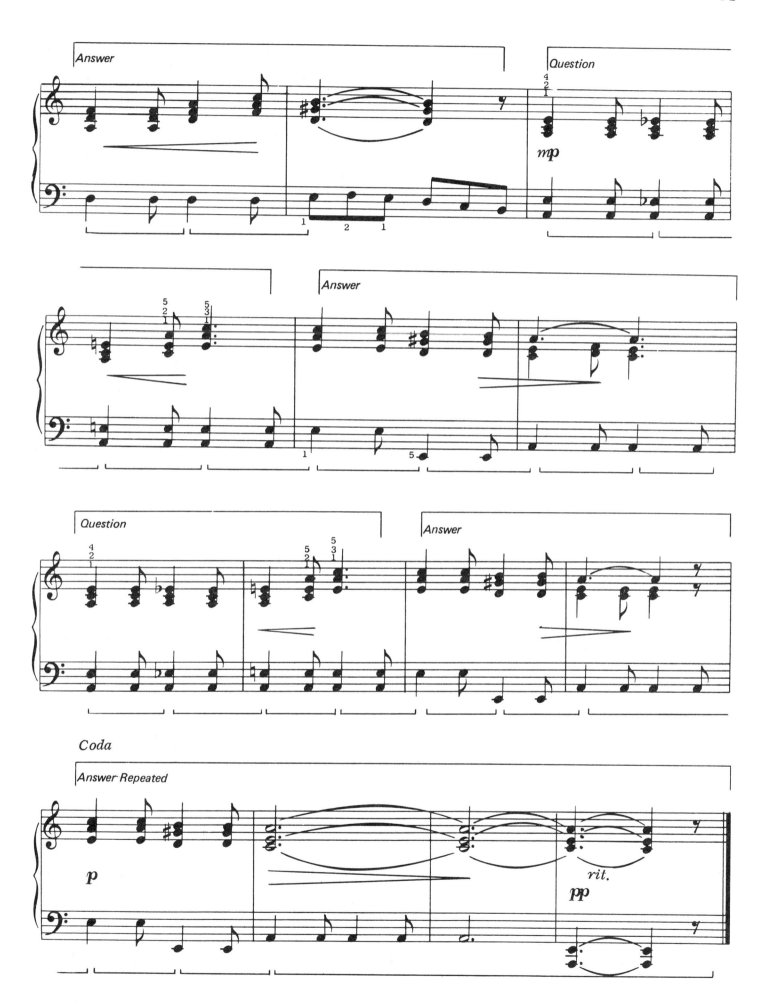

Chromatic Scale

A Chromatic Scale is a series of twelve successive half steps. It may begin or end on any note. It does not have a key signature.

Chromatic Studies

Teacher: Chromatic studies 1 and 2 may also be played together for ensemble practice.

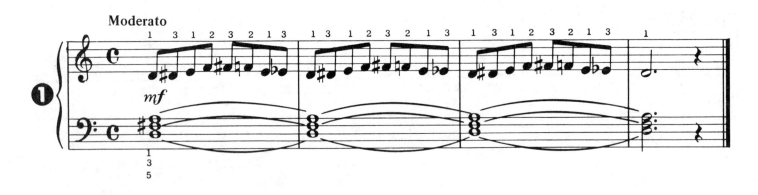

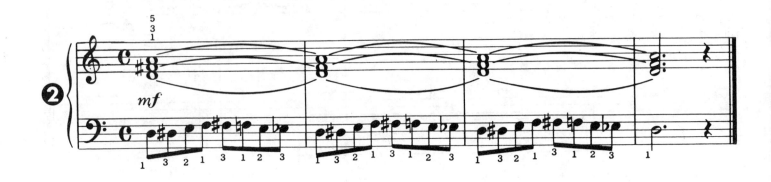

Chromatic Scale Ascending, Descending

Moderato

GLOVER

Chromatic Etude

GLOVER

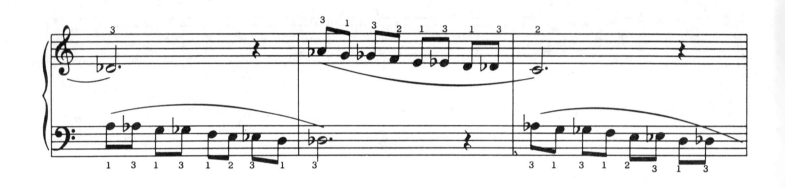

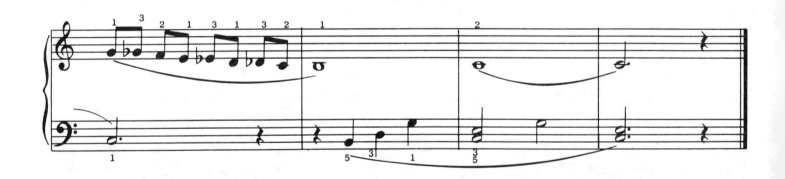

Night Winds

GLOVER

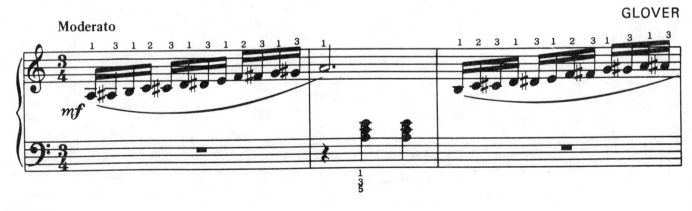

The Dotted Eighth Note

The dotted eighth note is equal in value to three sixteenth notes. It is usually followed by a sixteenth note. The two notes are equal to one quarter note.

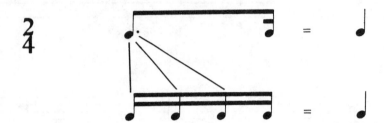

The dotted eighth note receives three-fourths of the beat and the sixteenth note receives one-fourth.

REMEMBER: *The dotted eighth note is three times longer than the sixteenth note.* Having the hands prepared for the note following the sixteenth note will assure moving on to the next beat in time.

Dotted Eighth Note Studies

I

II

Soldier Play

GLOVER

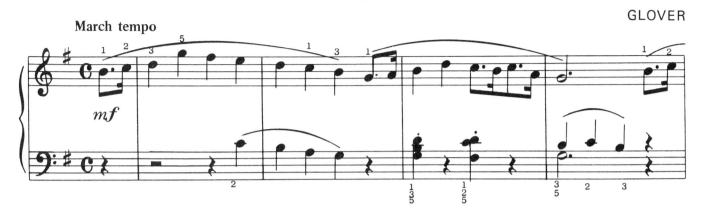

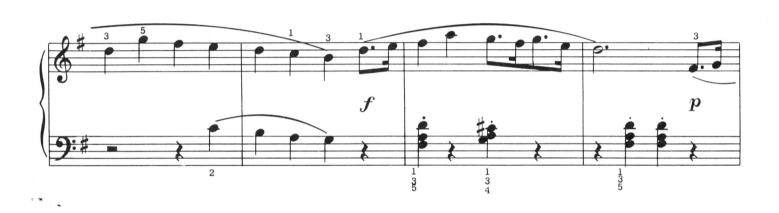

F.D.L.460

Longing

GURLITT

Dotted Eighth Note Studies

Teacher: *Eighth note studies 1* ⓐ *and* ⓑ *may also be played together for ensemble practice.*

Dotted Eighth Note Broken Triads, Contrary Motion

GLOVER

Dotted Eighth Note Tone Balance

GLOVER

F.D.L.460

Consecutive Inverted Triads, Dotted Eighth Note Rhythm

GLOVER

Teacher: Suggestions for ensemble performance. 1. Have some students play as written. 2. Have some students play both hand one octave higher.

F.D.L.460

Syncopation

When a long note is played on the weak part of the beat, the rhythm is syncopated. Clap and count the following rhythm pattern.

Syncopation Studies

I

Moderato

II

Moderato

Joshua Fit de Battle of Jericho

SPIRITUAL
arr. GLOVER

Lively

repeat R. H. 8va

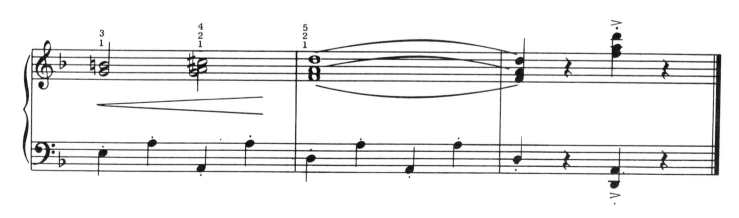

F.D.L.460

Pedro's Puppets

GLOVER

Syncopation

L. H. legato   (L.H. may be played one octave lower)

Teacher: Suggestions for ensemble performance. 1. Have some students play the right hand part with both hands one octave apart in unison. 2. Have some students plan the left hand part with both hands one octave apart in unison.

F.D.L.460

The Acciaccatura

The Acciaccatura, often referred to as a Grace Note, has no time value and is played very quickly before the principal note.

EARLY BIRD

LE COUPPEY

Sleigh Bells

Moving along but not fast

GLOVER

Bagatelle

Staccato

HUMMEL

Hold Tight

Finger Independence

GLOVER

Teacher: *It is recommended that Adult Repertoire, Level III-B, from the David Carr Glover Program for Adult Students be used at this time.*

Off They Go!

Rapid Five Finger Position and Scale Study

Allegro

BERENS

Major Arpeggios

When the notes of a Triad, as below, are played separately it is called an Arpeggio.

I

II

F.D.L.460

Minor Arpeggios

I

II

Teacher: It is recommended that Piano Arpeggios, Level 4, from the David Carr Glover Piano Library be used at this time.

Arpeggio Technic Studies

Arpeggio Half, Quarter, Eighth, Triplet, Sixteenth Notes, Two Octaves, Right Hand

Arpeggio Half, Quarter, Eighth, Triplet, Sixteenth Notes, Two Octaves, Left Hand

Arpeggio Contrary Motion

Arpeggio Ascending, Right Hand

Arpeggio Ascending, Left Hand

The Chase

GLOVER

F.D.L.460

Sonatina

There are many different kinds of compositions called Sonatina. The word Sonatina means a small Sonata. The Italian word Sonata means a piece that sounds on a musical instrument. Many Sonatinas and Sonatas developed during the classic period of music (from about 1770 to 1825) were based on a form known as the Sonata - Allegro Form. This you will learn more about later. Many other compositions bearing the name Sonatina that were composed before, during, and after the classic period were based on less involved forms such as Binary and Ternary.

The following Sonatina by Jacob Schmitt is an example of Ternary Form.

Sonatina

JACOB SCHMITT
(1803 – 1853)

Periods Of Music

BAROQUE PERIOD

The Baroque Period of music refers to music composed from approximately 1600 to 1750. On pages 59 through 64 will be found some of the music of Johann Sebastian Bach, German, (1685 – 1750), Domenico Scarlatti, Italian, (1685 – 1757), and George Frideric Handel, German, (1685 – 1759), all composers of the Baroque Period. Some of the other composers of this period not included in this book are: Jean-Baptiste Lully, French, (1632 – 1687); Henry Purcell, English, (1659 – 1695); Francois Couperin, French, (1668 – 1733); Georg Philipp Telemann, German, (1681 – 1767); Jean-Philippe Rameau, French, (1683 – 1764).

CLASSIC PERIOD

The Classic Period of music refers to music composed from approximately 1770 to 1825. On pages 65 - 74 will be found some of the music of Ludwig van Beethoven, German (1770 – 1827); Joseph Haydn, Austrian, (1732 – 1809); and Wolfgang Amadeus Mozart, Austrian, (1756 – 1791); all composers of the Classic Period. Also included are compositions by Leopold Mozart, Austrian, (1719 – 1787); and Johann Christoph Friedrich Bach, German, (1732 – 1795); both from the Rococo Period (transition period between Baroque and Classic). Some of the other composers of this period not included in this book are: Muzio Clementi, Italian, (1752 – 1832); Daniel Gottlob Türk, German, (1756 – 1813); Antonio Diabelli, Italian, (1781 – 1858); Friedrich Kuhlau, German, (1786 – 1832).

ROMANTIC PERIOD

The Romantic Period of music refers to music composed from approximately 1820 to 1900. On pages 75 through 78 will be found some of the music of Robert Schumann, German, (1810 – 1856) and Louis Köhler, German, (1820 – 1886), both composers of the Romantic Period. Some of the other composers of this period not included in this book are: Franz Schubert, Austrian, (1797 – 1828); Felix Mendelssohn, German, (1809 – 1847); Frédéric Chopin, Polish, (1810 – 1849); Franz Liszt, Hungarian, (1811 – 1886); César Franck, French, (1822 – 1890); Johannes Brahms, German, (1833 – 1897); Peter Ilyich Tchaikovsky, Russian, (1840 – 1893); Edvard Grieg, Norwegian, (1843 – 1907).

CONTEMPORARY PERIOD

The Contemporary Period of music refers to music composed from approximately 1900 to today. On pages 79 through 83 will be found some of the music of Alexander Grechaninov, Russian, (1864 – 1956), Béla Bartók, Hungarian, (1881 – 1945) and Dmitry Kabalevsky, Russian, (1904 –   ), all composers of the Contemporary Period. Some of the other composers of this period not included in this book are: Claude Debussy, French, (1862 – 1918); Sergey Rachmaninoff, Russian, (1873 – 1943); Arnold Schoenberg, Austrian, (1874 – 1951); Maurice Ravel, French, (1875 – 1937); Heitor Villa-Lobos, Brazilian, (1887 – 1959); Igor Stravinsky, Russian, (1882 –   ); Sergey Prokofiev, Russian, (1891 – 1953); Darius Milhaud, French, (1892 –   ); Paul Hindemith, German, (1895 – 1963); George Gershwin, American, (1898 – 1937); Alexander Tcherepnin, Russian, (1899 –   ); Aaron Copland, American, (1900 –   ); Aram Khachaturian, Russian, (1903 –   ); Dimitry Shostakovich, Russian, (1906 –   ); Samuel Barber, American, (1910 –   ); Norman Dello Joio, American, (1913 –   ).

SONGS FOR SPECIAL OCCASIONS

On pages 84 through 86 will be found songs for special occasions. All have been modified to fit the degree of advancement of the student who will find them useful. In time, when the student's technic is developed, it is suggested that the originals of these songs be used.

When the Time Signature **C** (**4/4**) appears with a line **₵** it is called Alla Breve. It means to count two beats for each measure and the half note receives one beat. It is also referred to as Cut Time.

Musette

JOHANN SEBASTIAN BACH
(1685 — 1750)

Prelude

Baroque Period 1600-1750

JOHANN SEBASTIAN BACH
(1685 — 1750)

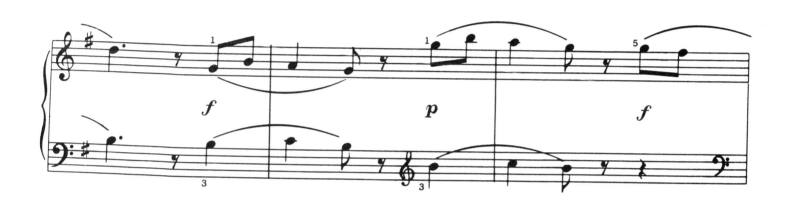

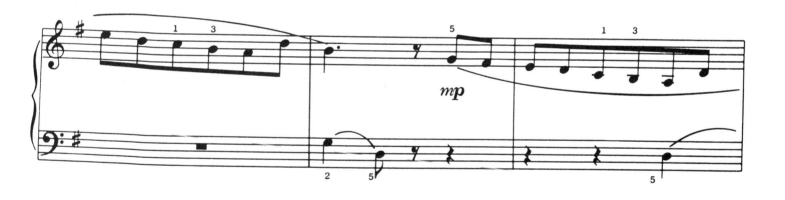

F.D.L.460

Chorale

Baroque Period 1600-1750

JOHANN SEBASTIAN BACH
(1685 – 1750)

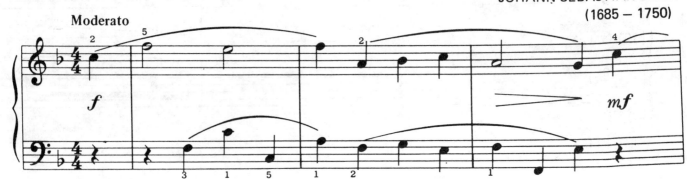

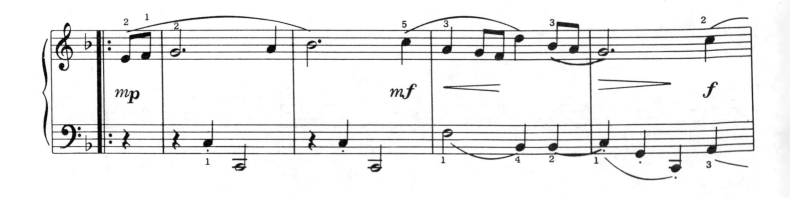

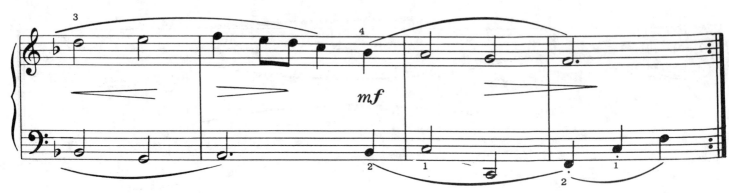

Minuet from Suite in C Minor

Baroque Period 1600-1750

DOMENICO SCARLATTI
(1685 – 1757)

Allegretto

F.D.L.460

In **3/8** rhythm there are three beats to each measure and an eighth note receives one beat. This rhythm is slightly faster and often a lighter feeling than **3/4** .

Minuet

GEORGE FRIDERIC HANDEL
(1685 — 1759)

Baroque Period 1600-1750

Minuet in F

Rococo Period

*LEOPOLD MOZART
1719 – 1787

Moderato

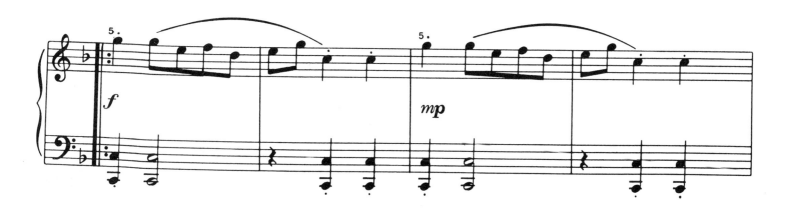

The father of Wolfgang Amadeus Mozart.

F.D.L.460

Air

Rococo Period

* JOHANN CHRISTOPH FRIEDRICH BACH
(1732 – 1795)

*The sixteenth child and ninth son of Johann Sebastian Bach.

Russian Folk Dance

Classic Period 1770-1825

Lively

LUDWIG van BEETHOVEN
1770 — 1827

German Dance

Classic Period 1770-1825

LUDWIG van BEETHOVEN
1770 — 1827

Country Dance

Classic Period 1770-1825

LUDWIG van BEETHOVEN
1770 — 1827

Andante

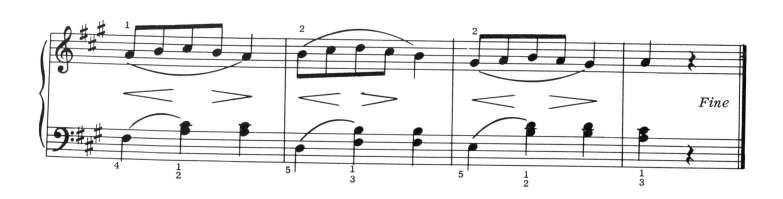

Practice the left hand separately until the sustained bass voice is under control.

Quick Dance

Classic Period 1770-1825

JOSEPH HAYDN
1732 — 1809

F.D.L.460

Minuet in F

Classic Period 1770-1825

WOLFGANG AMADEUS MOZART
1756 – 1791

Minuet in C

Classic Period 1770-1825

WOLFGANG AMADEUS MOZART
1756 — 1791

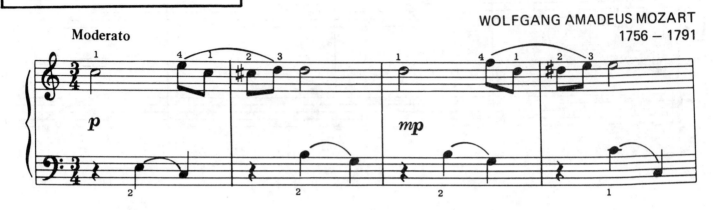

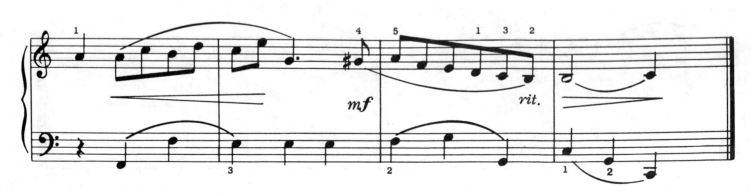

Soldier's March

Romantic Period 1800-1900

ROBERT SCHUMANN
1810 — 1856

The Wild Horseman

Romantic Period 1800-1900

ROBERT SCHUMANN
1810 – 1856

Melody

Romantic Period 1800-1900

ROBERT SCHUMANN
1810 – 1856

Andante (not fast)

F.D.L.460

In The Church

Romantic Period 1800-1900

LOUIS KÖHLER
1820 – 1886

Promenade

Contemporary Period 1900

ALEXANDER GRECHANINOV
1864 – 1956

Folk Song

BÉLA BARTÓK
1881 — 1945

Contemporary Period 1900

Allegro

Toccatina

Contemporary Period 1900

DMITRY KABALEVSKY
1904 —

America The Beautiful

Katharine Lee Bates

SAMUEL A. WARD

The Star-Spangled Banner

Music For
Special Occasions

Francis Scott Key

JOHN STAFFORD SMITH

America

Samuel F. Smith

HENRY CAREY

Birthday Song

Traditional

Major Arpeggio Dictionary

F.D.L.460

88

A MAJOR
Root Position

First Inversion

Second Inversion

E MAJOR
Root Position

First Inversion

Second Inversion

B MAJOR
Root Postion

First Inversion

Second Inversion

F.D.L.460

89

F.D.L.460

90

Minor Arpeggio Dictionary

F# MINOR
Root Position

First Inversion

Second Inversion

C# MINOR
Root Position

First Inversion

Second Inversion

G# MINOR
Root Position

First Inversion

Second Inversion

D# MINOR
Root Position

First Inversion   Second Inversion

A# MINOR
Root Position

First Inversion   Second Inversion

D MINOR
Root Position

First Inversion   Second Inversion